EASY ACCESSORIES

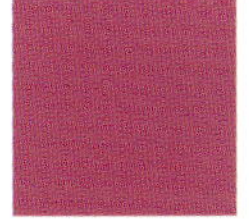

Let your imagination run free with Fun Fur by Lion Brand® Yarn Company. This easy-to-use novelty "eyelash" yarn is available in solids or prints and can be used as trim or to create entire projects. Fun Fur is also an ideal "mixing" yarn — try combining it with Homespun®, like we did for these twelve designs, or with another of your favorite yarns when you want to make a quick project on large needles or hooks. Just hold one or more strands of Fun Fur with one or more strands of the other yarn.

Fun Fur is a 100% polyester yarn, machine washable and is available in solids and prints. Solid balls weigh 1.75 oz (50 grams) and are 60 yds (54 meters) long, while print balls have a weight of 1.5 oz (40 grams) and a yardage of 57 yds (52 meters). For the knitting gauge, 16 stitches and 20 rows should equal 4" (10 cm) on size 10.5 (6.5 mm) needles. For the crochet gauge, 12 single crochet and 14 rows should equal 4" (10 cm) on a size K-10.5 (6.5 mm) hook.

Homespun® is a bulky-weight, richly textured 98% acrylic-2% polyester blend. It weighs 6 oz (170 grams) per skein and has a length of 185 yds (167 meters). For the knitting gauge, 14 stitches and 20 rows should equal 4" (10 cm) on size 10 (6 mm) needles. For the crochet gauge, 10 single crochet and 10 rows should equal 4" (10 cm) on a size K-10.5 (6.5 mm) hook.

GENERAL INSTRUCTIONS

ABBREVIATIONS

CC	Contrasting Color
ch(s)	chain(s)
cm	centimeters
cont	continu(e)(ing)
hdc	half double crochet
inc	increas(e)(s)(ing)
k	knit
MC	Main Color
p	purl
rem	remain(s)(ing)
rep	repeat(s)(ing)
Rnd(s)	Round(s)
RS	Right side
sc	single crochet(s)
st(s)	stitch(es)
tbl	through back loop(s)
tog	together
WS	Wrong side
yo	yarn over

* — When you see an asterisk used within a pattern row, the symbol indicates that later you will be told to repeat a portion of the instruction. Most often the instructions will say, repeat from * so many times.

** or *** — Used to set off a block of text. Look for direction, such as: repeat between **'s or ***'s so many times.

( ) or [ ] — Set off a short number of stitches that are repeated a series of times. For example: [2 sc, 2 dc, 2 sc in next stitch] twice.

GAUGE

Never underestimate the importance of gauge. Achieving the correct gauge assures that the finished size of your piece matches the finished size given in the pattern.

CHECKING YOUR GAUGE

Work a swatch that is at least 4″ (10 cm) square. Use the suggested hook or needle size and the number of stitches given. For example, the standard LION BRAND® Fun Fur knit gauge is: 16 sts + 20 rows = 4″ (10 cm) on size 10½ (6.5 mm) needles. If your swatch is larger than 4″, you need to work it again using smaller needles; if it is smaller than 4″, try it with larger needles. The same process applies to crochet hooks. This might require a swatch or two to get the exact gauge given in the pattern.

METRICS

As a handy reference, keep in mind that 1 ounce = approximately 28 grams and 1″ = 2.5 centimeters.

TERMS

continue in this way or as established — Once a pattern is set up (established), the instructions may tell you to continue in the same way.

fasten off — To end your piece, you need to simply pull the yarn through the last loop left on the hook. This keeps the last stitch intact and prevents the work from unraveling.

right side — Refers to the front of the piece.

work even — This is used to indicate an area worked as established without increasing or decreasing.

wrong side — Refers to the back of the piece.

CROCHET TERMINOLOGY	
UNITED STATES	**INTERNATIONAL**
slip stitch (slip st) =	single crochet (sc)
single crochet (sc) =	double crochet (dc)
half double crochet (hdc) =	half treble crochet (htr)
double crochet (dc) =	treble crochet (tr)
treble crochet (tr) =	double treble crochet (dtr)
double treble crochet (dtr) =	triple treble crochet (ttr)
triple treble crochet (tr tr) =	quadruple treble crochet (qtr)
skip =	miss

ALUMINUM CROCHET HOOKS													
U.S.	B-1	C-2	D-3	E-4	F-5	G-6	H-8	I-9	J-10	K-10½	N	P	Q
Metric - mm	2.25	2.75	3.25	3.5	3.75	4	5	5.5	6	6.5	9	10	15

KNIT TERMINOLOGY	
UNITED STATES	**INTERNATIONAL**
gauge =	tension
bind off =	cast off
yarn over (yo) =	yarn forward (yfwd) **or** yarn around needle (yrn)

KNITTING NEEDLES																
U.S.	0	1	2	3	4	5	6	7	8	9	10	10½	11	13	15	17
Metric - mm	2	2.25	2.75	3.25	3.5	3.75	4	4.5	5	5.5	6	6.5	8	9	10	12.75

BEGINNER	Projects for first-time crocheters using basic stitches. Minimal shaping.
EASY	Projects using yarn with basic stitches, repetitive stitch patterns, simple color changes, and simple shaping and finishing.
INTERMEDIATE	Projects using a variety of techniques, such as basic lace patterns or color patterns, mid-level shaping and finishing.
EXPERIENCED	Projects with intricate stitch patterns, techniques and dimension, such as non-repeating patterns, multi-color techniques, fine threads, small hooks, detailed shaping and refined finishing.

Yarn Weight Symbol & Names	SUPER FINE 1	FINE 2	LIGHT 3	MEDIUM 4	BULKY 5	SUPER BULKY 6
Type of Yarns in Category	Sock, Fingering, Baby	Sport, Baby	DK, Light Worsted	Worsted, Afghan, Aran	Chunky, Craft, Rug	Bulky, Roving

BASIC CROCHET STITCHES & TECHNIQUES

CHAIN *(abbreviated ch)*

To work a chain stitch, begin with a slip knot on the hook. Bring the yarn **over** hook from back to front, catching the yarn with the hook and turning the hook slightly toward you to keep the yarn from slipping off. Draw the yarn through the slip knot ***(Fig. 1)***. Continue drawing loops through until you have the number of chains stated in pattern.

Fig. 1

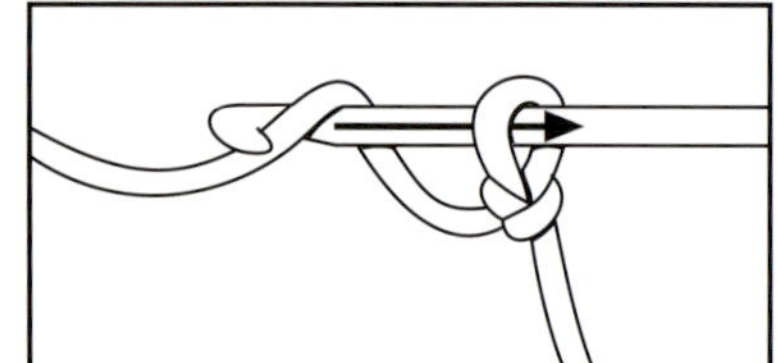

WORKING INTO THE CHAIN

Method 1: Insert hook into back ridge of each chain ***(Fig. 2a)***.

Method 2: Insert hook under top two strands of each chain ***(Fig. 2b)***.

Fig. 2a

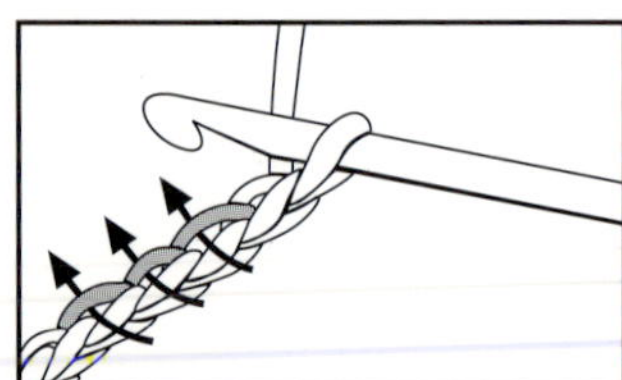

Fig. 2b

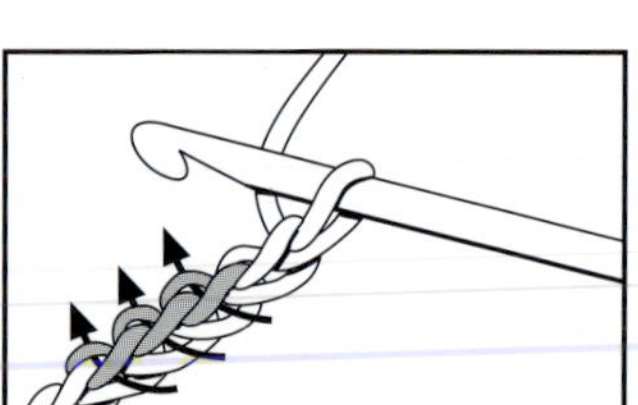

SLIP STITCH *(abbreviated slip st)*

To work a slip stitch, insert hook in stitch indicated, yo and draw through st and through loop on hook ***(Fig. 3)***.

Fig. 3

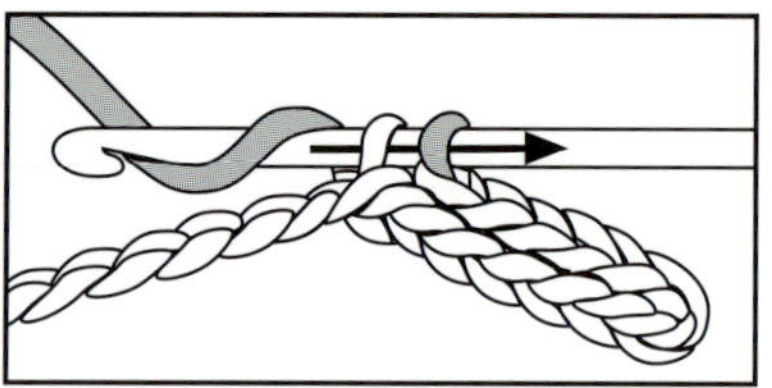

SINGLE CROCHET *(abbreviated sc)*

Insert hook in stitch indicated, yo and pull up a loop, yo and draw through both loops on hook ***(Fig. 4)***.

Fig. 4

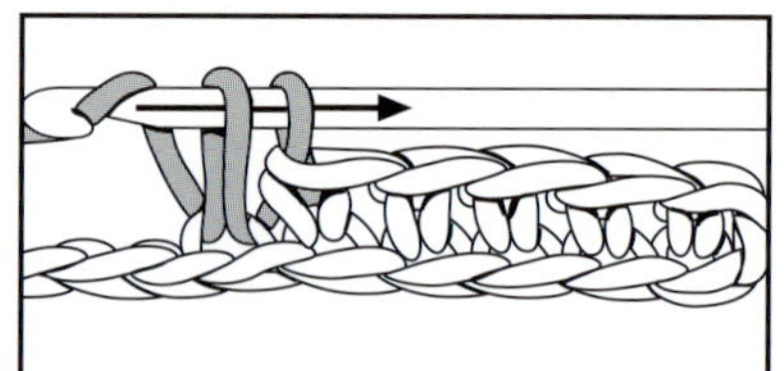

HALF DOUBLE CROCHET

(abbreviated hdc)

Yo, insert hook in stitch indicated, yo and pull up a loop, yo and draw through all 3 loops on hook ***(Fig. 5)***.

Fig. 5

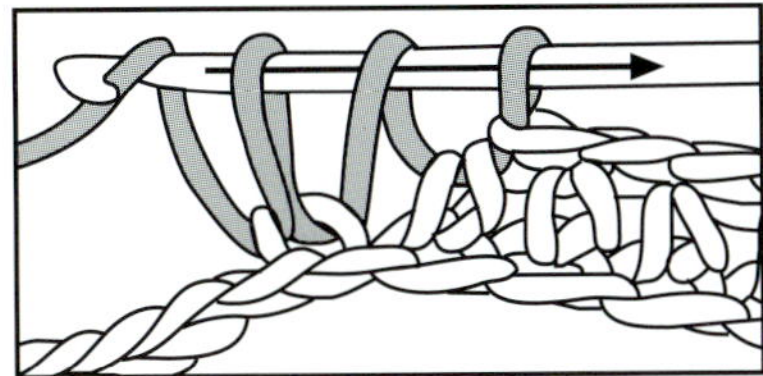

TREBLE CROCHET

(abbreviated tr)

Yo twice, insert hook in stitch indicated, yo and pull up a loop (4 loops on hook) ***(Fig. 6a)***, (yo and draw through 2 loops on hook) 3 times ***(Fig. 6b)***.

Fig. 6a

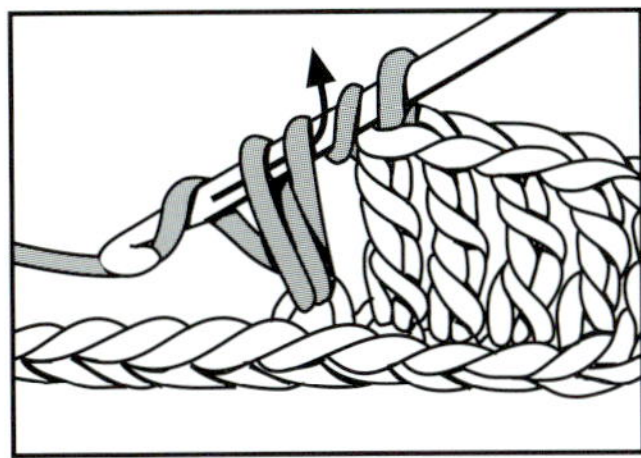

Fig. 6b

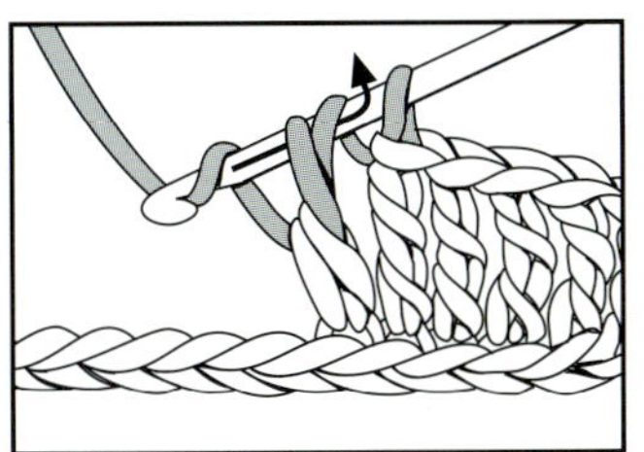

BASIC KNIT STITCHES

STOCKINETTE STITCH

Knit one row or number of stitches indicated (right side), purl one row or number of stitches indicated. The knit side is smooth and flat ***(Fig. 7a)***, and the purl side is bumpy ***(Fig. 7b)***.

Fig. 7a

Fig. 7b

GARTER STITCH

Knit every row. Two rows of knitting make one horizontal ridge in your fabric ***(Fig. 8)***.

Fig. 8

KNIT INCREASE

Knit the next stitch but do **not** slip the old stitch off the left needle ***(Fig. 9a)***. Insert the right needle into the **back** loop of the **same** stitch and knit it ***(Fig. 9b)***, then slip the old stitch off the left needle.

Fig. 9a

Fig. 9b

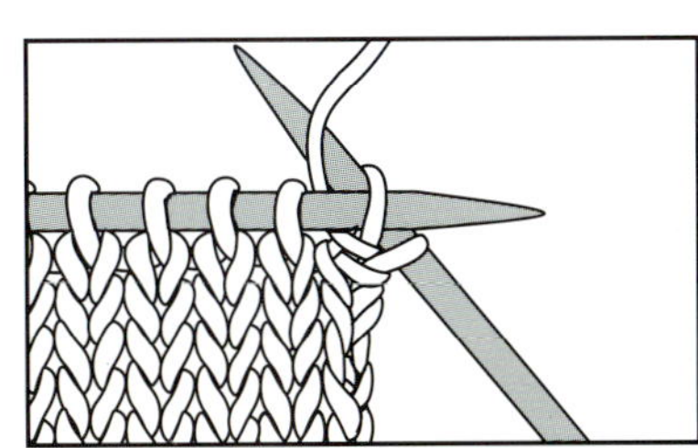

KNIT 2 TOGETHER

(abbreviated k2tog)

Insert the right needle into the **front** of the first two stitches on the left needle as if to **knit** ***(Fig. 10)***, then **knit** them together as if they were one stitch.

Fig. 10

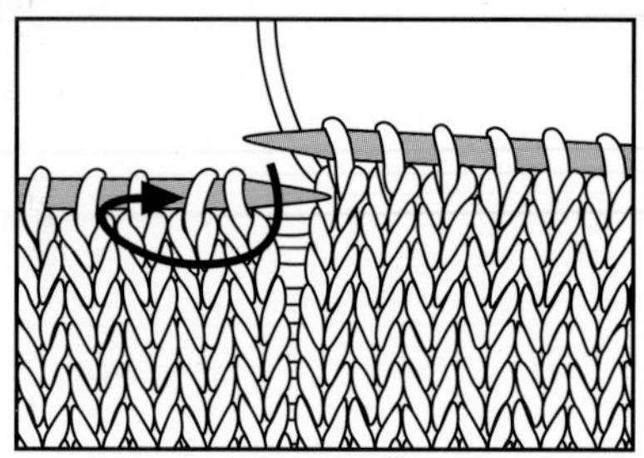

KNIT 2 TOGETHER TBL

(abbreviated k2tog tbl)

Insert the right needle from **front** to **back** of the first two stitches on the left needle and then **knit** them together as if they were one stitch ***(Fig. 11)***.

Fig. 11

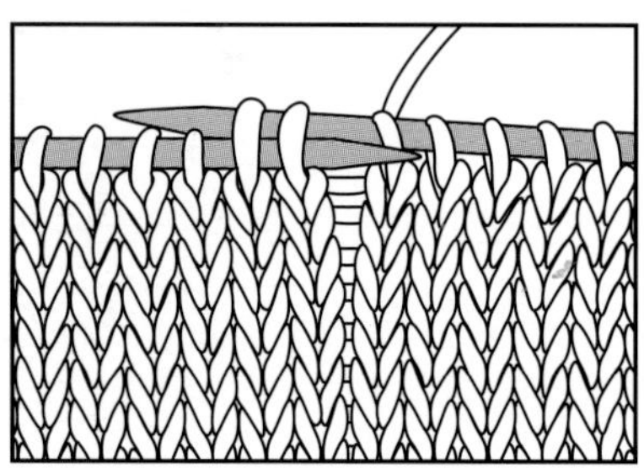

KNIT 3 TOGETHER

(abbreviated k3tog)

Insert the right needle into the **front** of the first three stitches on the left needle as if to **knit** ***(Fig. 12)***, then **knit** them together as if they were one stitch.

Fig. 12

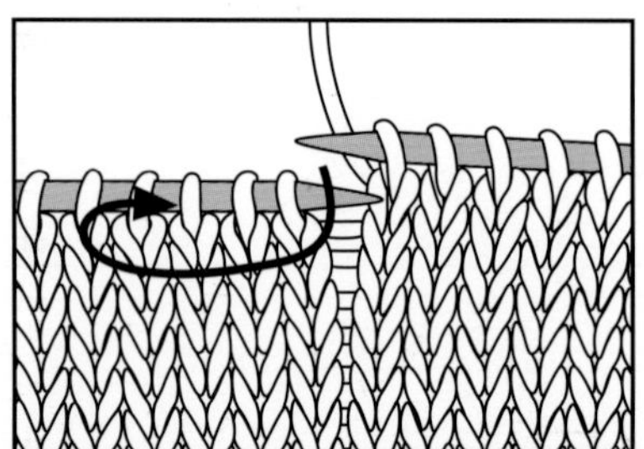

YARN OVER

After a knit stitch, before a knit stitch

Bring the yarn forward **between** the needles, then back **over** the top of the right hand needle, so that it is now in position to knit the next stitch ***(Fig. 13)***.

Fig. 13

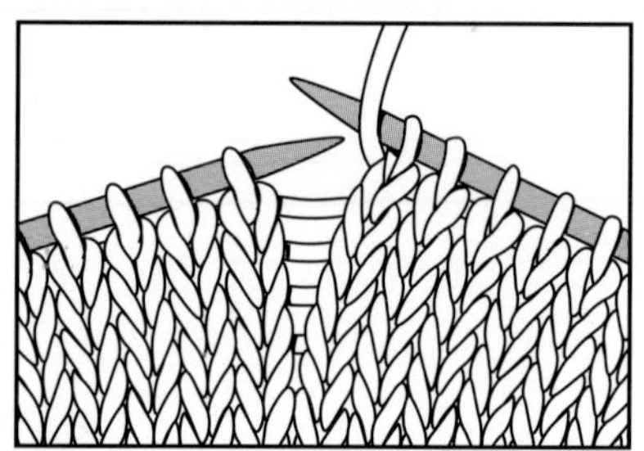

TASSEL

Cut a piece of cardboard 5″ (12.5 cm) wide and wrap yarn around the cardboard 24 times. Cut an 24″ (61 cm) length of yarn and insert it under all of the strands at the top of the cardboard; pull up **tightly** and tie securely. Leave the yarn ends long enough to attach the tassel. Cut the yarn at the opposite end of the cardboard and then remove it ***(Fig. 14a)***. Cut a 6″ (15.25 cm) length of yarn and wrap it **tightly** around the tassel twice, 1″ (2.5 cm) below the top ***(Fig. 14b)***; tie securely. Trim the ends.

Fig. 14a

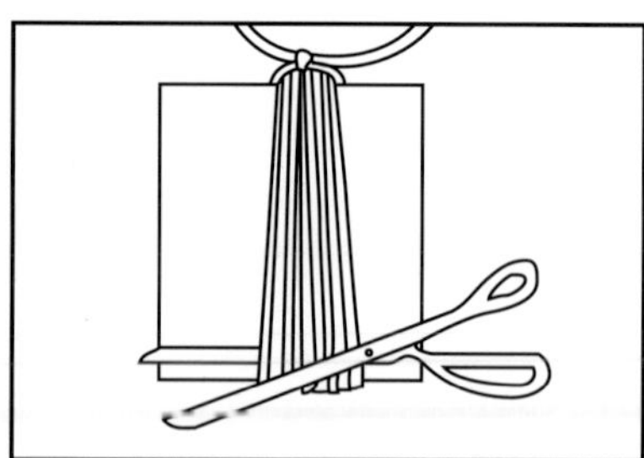

Fig. 14b

Crochet Water Bottle Carrier

Finished size: 8″ x 11″
(20 cm x 28 cm)

MATERIALS

BULKY 5

- LION BRAND® Homespun® #364 Mexicana (MC) - 1 skein

BULKY 5

- LION BRAND® Fun Fur #191 Violet (CC) - 1 ball or colors of your choice
- Crochet hook size J-10 (6 mm) or size needed for gauge
- Large-eyed, blunt needle

GAUGE: 11 sts = 4″ (10 cm) in single crochet with MC.

CARRIER

With MC, ch 2.

Rnd 1: Work 6 sc in 2nd ch from hook, mark beginning of rnd.

Rnds 2-5: Continue in sc, inc 6 sts each rnd evenly spaced.

Continue working even on 30 sts for 8″. Switch to 2 strands of CC and work 5 rnds even, fasten off.

STRAP

With MC ch for 36″, turn and work 1 row slip st, fasten off.

FINISHING

Sew strap to bottle holder at inside edges. Weave in ends.

Knit Diagonal Scarf

Finished Size: $65^1/_2$″ x $5^1/_2$″
(166.25 cm x 14 cm)

EASY

MATERIALS

BULKY 5

- LION BRAND® Homespun® #302 Colonial (MC) - 1 skein

BULKY 5

- LION BRAND® Fun Fur #191 Violet (CC) - 1 ball or colors of your choice
- Knitting needles size 10 (6 mm) or size to obtain gauge

GAUGE: 12 sts and 24 rows = 4″ (10 cm) in Garter St (knit every row) with MC

NOTE

When working rows with only MC, weave CC along edge as you go.

SCARF

With MC, cast on 24 sts.

Row 1: Knit.

Row 2: K 1, inc 1, k across to last 2 sts, k2tog.

Repeat last 2 rows 3 more times.

Continuing to work in pattern as established, add in a strand of CC and work for 5 rows.

Repeat last 13 rows 14 more times. Work 8 more rows in MC only. Bind off all sts.

FINISHING

For each tassel, cut 15″ strands: 12 of MC and 6 of CC. Pull through end of scarf, tie in an overhand knot and trim. Repeat for other end.

CROCHETED HAT

Finished Size: 21″ (53.5 cm) circumference
One size fits most adults

 EASY

MATERIALS

- LION BRAND® Homespun® #319 Adirondack (MC) - 1 skein
- LION BRAND® Fun Fur #134 Copper (CC) - 1 ball or colors of your choice
- Crochet hook size J-10 (6 mm) or size needed for gauge
- 5″ piece of cardboard

BULKY 5

BULKY 5

GAUGE: 12 sts = 4″ (10 cm) in single crochet with 1 strand each MC and CC held together.

HAT

With 1 strand each of MC and CC held together, ch 64. Being careful not to twist ch, begin working sc in first ch to form a loop.

Rnds 1-7: Sc in each ch around with 1 strand each of MC and CC. Drop CC.

Rnds 8-12: Sc in each sc around with 1 strand MC. Pick up CC.

Rnd 13: Sc in each sc around with 1 strand each of MC and CC.

Repeat Rnds 8-13 twice more. Drop CC and work 3 rnds with MC.

FINISHING

Sew across top, bring 2 points together and tack in place.

TASSEL

Wrap MC around cardboard 24 times. Cut 24″ length of yarn, fold it in half, and thread through top of Tassel and tie tightly. Cut other end open to remove cardboard. Using another length of yarn folded in half, wrap yarn around Tassel tightly several times about 1″ below top knot.
Make a 3″ long, 6-strand braid and attach to top of Hat with Tassel at end.

WAVY FUR WRAP

Finished size: 10″ x 48″
(25.5 cm x 122 cm)

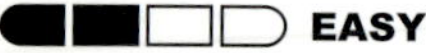 EASY

MATERIALS

BULKY 5

- LION BRAND® Fun Fur
  #113 Red (A) - 1 ball
  #209 Mango (B) - 1 ball
  #195 Hot Pink (C) - 1 ball
  or colors of your choice
- Knitting needles size 11 (8 mm) or size needed for gauge

GAUGE: 12 sts and 24 rows = 4″ (10 cm) in Garter St (knit every row)

NOTE
Always leave a 6″ tail when cutting/joining yarn

WRAP

With A, cast on 123 sts.

Rows 1 and 2: Knit.

Row 3: K 2, (k2tog) 3 times, *(yo, k 1) 5 times, yo, (k2tog) 6 times, repeat from * 5 times more, (yo, k 1) 5 times, yo, (k2tog) 3 times, k 2.

Cut A and start B, repeat last 3 rows with B.

Cut B and start C, work last 3 rows with C.

Continue in this manner until 12 stripes completed. Bind off loosely.

FINISHING

Cut several 12″ lengths of A, B, and C. Knot in with tails for fringe by pairing new strand pulled through and doubled with strands of each of other colors from tails and knotting all 4 strands in an overhand knot.

Crochet Loopy Boa

Finished size: 56″ (142.25 cm) long

BEGINNER

MATERIALS

BULKY 5

- LION BRAND® Fun Fur #207 Citrus - 2 balls or color of your choice
- Crochet hook size N-13 (9 mm) or size needed for gauge
- Large-eyed, blunt needle

GAUGE: Gauge does not matter for this project.

BOA

With 2 strands of yarn held together, *chain 10, slip stitch in first chain to form a loop; repeat from *, making loops until approximately 3 yards of yarn remain. Fold boa in half and sew together.

Knit Tote

Finished size: 9″ x 9″
(23.75 cm x 23.75 cm)

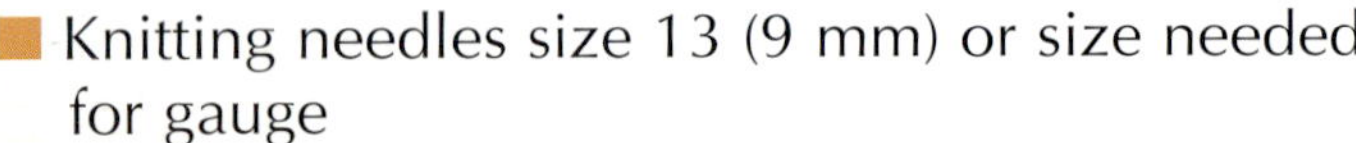

MATERIALS

- LION BRAND® Homespun® #360 Mardi Gras (MC) - 1 skein
- LION BRAND® Fun Fur #109 Sapphire (CC) - 1 ball or colors of your choice
- Knitting needles size 13 (9 mm) or size needed for gauge
- Large-eyed, blunt needle

BULKY 5

BULKY 5

GAUGE: 9 stitches and 16 rows = 4″ (10 cm) in Garter Stitch (knit every row) with 2 strands MC held together

SIDE — Make 2

With 2 strands of MC held together, cast on 21 stitches. Work 36 rows in Garter Stitch. Change to 2 strands of CC, work 8 rows Garter Stitch. Bind off loosely.

STRAP — Make 2

With 2 strands of MC held together, cast on 3 stitches.

Row 1: Slip 1, knit 2.

Repeat Row 1 until Strap measures 18″, Bind off.

FINISHING

Sew side and bottom seams. Push bottom corners in making a fold perpendicular to the side and bottom seams – creating a flat bottom. Tack in place, Sew on straps.

Crochet Scrunchie

BEGINNER

MATERIALS

BULKY 5

- LION BRAND® Fun Fur #208 Tropical - 1 ball or color of your choice
- Crochet hook size K-10½ (6.5 mm)
- One large elastic-coated hair band

GAUGE: Gauge does not matter in this pattern.

SCRUNCHIE

Join yarn to hair band. Work 60 treble crochets into hairband. Fasten off and weave in end.

Cell Phone or Sunglasses Holder

Finished Size: 3″ x 5″
(7.5 cm x 12.75 cm)

BEGINNER

MATERIALS

BULKY 5

- LION BRAND® Fun Fur #203 Indigo - 1 ball or color of your choice
- Knitting needles size 10 (6 mm) or size needed for gauge
- Crochet hook size J-10 (6 mm)
- Large-eyed, blunt needle

GAUGE: 16 stitches and 32 rows = 4″ (10 cm) in Garter Stitch (knit every row)

CASE

With 2 strands of yarn held together, cast on 12 stitches. Work 12″ in Garter Stitch. Bind off.

Fold piece to create a 5″ pouch with a 2″ overlapping flap. Sew side seams through all thicknesses. With crochet hook, make a chain 18″ long. Knot and trim ends. Weave strap through top of bag at base of flap. Tie ends together to attach to your purse strap.

Bias Keyhole Scarf

Finished Size: 30″ x 4¾″
(76 cm x 12 cm)

EASY

MATERIALS

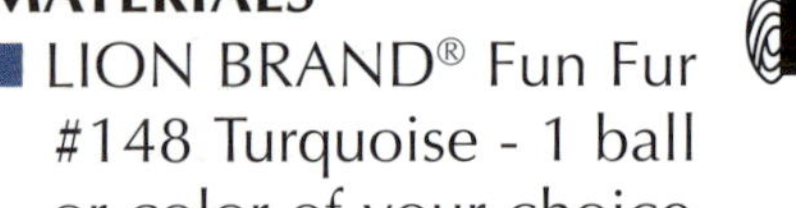

- LION BRAND® Fun Fur #148 Turquoise - 1 ball or color of your choice
- Knitting needles size 10 (6 mm) or size needed for gauge

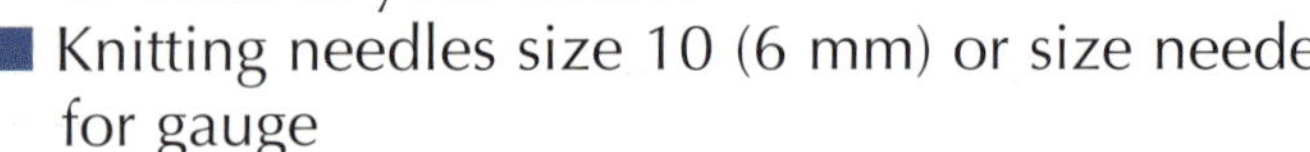

GAUGE: 12 sts and 16 rows = 4″ (10 cm) in Garter st (knit every row)

SCARF

Cast on 20 sts.

Row 1 Knit.

Row 2 K 1, inc 1, k across to last 2 sts, k2tog.

Repeat last 2 rows 3 more times.

Continue to work in pattern as established until piece measures 24″ from beginning.

Next Row Keeping in pattern, bind off center two sts.

Next Row Keeping in pattern, cast on 2 across center two sts.

Continue to work in pattern as established, until piece measures 30″ from beginning, or 2 yards of yarn remain. Bind off all sts.

Boa

Finished Size: 5″ x 62″
(12.75 cm x 157.5 cm)

EASY

MATERIALS

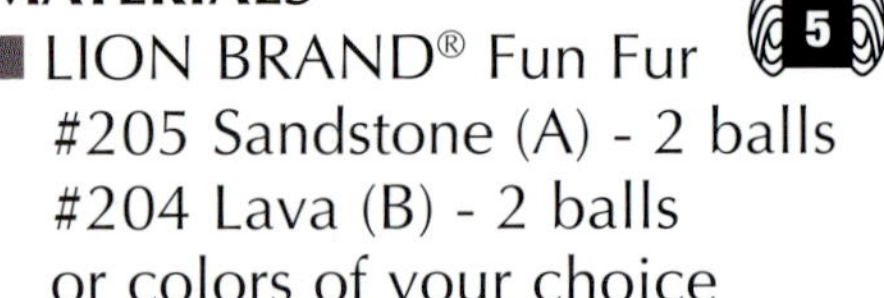

- LION BRAND® Fun Fur
  #205 Sandstone (A) - 2 balls
  #204 Lava (B) - 2 balls
  or colors of your choice
- Knitting needles size 11 (8 mm) or size needed for gauge

GAUGE: 16 sts = 4″ (10 cm) in Garter st (knit every row).

NOTES
When changing colors, be sure to twist yarns from underneath to avoid holes. Cut and join yarn as needed.
Boa is worked on the diagonal in Garter st.

Color Sequence
(6 rows A; 4 rows B) 2 times; 6 rows A; 14 rows B.

BOA

HORIZONTAL SHAPING

With A, cast on 1 st.

Row 1 (RS): K 1, p 1, k 1 into st (inc 2 made). 3 sts.
Row 2: Knit.
Row 3: (K 1, p 1) into st (inc 1 made), k 1, inc 1. 5 sts.
Row 4: Knit.
Row 5: Inc 1, k across to last 2 sts, inc 1, k 1.
Row 6: Knit.

Repeat Rows 5 and 6, cont in Color Sequence with 4 rows B.

AT SAME TIME, when there are 27 sts on needle, ending with a Row 6;

BEGIN VERTICAL PATTERN

Keeping in Color Sequence, cont as follows:

Row 7 (RS): K2tog tbl, k across to last 2 sts, inc 1, k 1.

Row 8: Knit.

Repeat Rows 7 and 8 until 5 repeats of Color Sequence have been completed (the 5th wide band of B has been worked, ending with a Row 8).

BEGIN END HORIZONTAL SHAPING

Keeping in Color Sequence, cont as follows:

Row 9 (RS): With A, k2tog tbl, k to last 2 sts, k2tog.

Row 10: Knit.

Repeat Rows 9 and 10 until 3 sts rem. On next WS row k 3, then k3tog on following RS row. Bind off and weave in ends.

Knit Bias Bag

Finished Size: 12″ x 10″
(30.5 cm x 25.5 cm)

EASY

MATERIALS

BULKY 5

- LION BRAND® Homespun® #312 Edwardian (MC) - 1 skein
- LION BRAND® Fun Fur #134 Copper (CC) - 1 ball or colors of your choice
- Knitting needles size 10 (6 mm) or size needed for gauge
- Large-eyed, blunt needle

GAUGE: 12 sts and 24 rows = 4″ (10 cm) in Garter Stitch (knit every row) with MC

NOTE
When working rows with only MC, weave CC along edge as you go.

BAG

With MC, cast on 48 sts.

Row 1: Knit.

Row 2: K 1, inc 1, k across to last 2 sts, k2tog. Repeat last 2 rows 3 more times.

Continuing to work in pattern as established, add in a strand of CC and work for 5 rows.

Repeat last 13 rows 5 more times. Bind off all sts.

STRAP

With 2 strands of MC held tog, cast on 3 sts.

Row 1: Slip 1, k 2.

Repeat Row 1 until Strap measures 60″, bind off.

FINISHING

With 2 strands of CC held tog, pick up 78 sts along one side edge of piece (across ends of rows). Knit 5 rows, bind off all sts. Fold bag, matching the cast on and bind off edges. Sew tog into a tube, sew bottom seam. Sew strap to Bag on the inside, extending straps to the bottom of bag for stability.

Crochet Ear Warmers

One size fits most adults

EASY

MATERIALS

BULKY 5

- LION BRAND® Homespun® #302 Colonial (MC) - 1 skein
- LION BRAND® Fun Fur #203 Indigo (CC) - 1 ball or colors of your choice
- Crochet hook size N-13 (9 mm) or size needed for gauge
- Large-eyed, blunt needle

GAUGE: Does not matter in this pattern.

EAR — Make 2

With 1 strand each of MC and CC held together, chain 2.

Rnd 1: Work 7 sc in 2nd chain from hook, mark beginning of rnd.

Rnds 2-4: Continue in sc, increasing 7 sts each rnd evenly spaced. 28 sc, drop MC.

Rnd 5: With CC only work around in sc. Fasten off.

BAND

With MC, ch 21.

Rnd 1: Sc in 2nd ch from hook and in each ch across to last ch, 3 sc in last ch; continuing along bottom of foundation ch, work 19 sc, work 3 sc in last ch. 44 sts.

Rnd 2: Work * 4 slip st, 4 sc, 5 hdc, 4 sc, 4 slip st, 2 sc in end st, repeat from *. 46 sts.

Rnd 3: Work * 21 sc, 2 sc in each of next 2 sts, repeat from *. 50 sts.

Rnd 4: Change to CC and work around in sc. Fasten off.

FINISHING

Pin ears to band and try on for fit. Adjust and sew ears to band. **Ties:** Cut three 36″ lengths of MC, pull through at bottom edge of one ear, line up ends and tie in an overhand knot at ear. Divide strands into three groups of 2, braid to end, finish in an overhand knot, trim ends. Repeat for other side.

DESIGNERS

LINDA CYR

STITCHWORX

Production Team
Editorial Director, Lion Brand - Nancy Thomas
Editorial Writer - Kimber Ross
Graphic Artist - Amy Gerke
Lead Graphic Artist - Rebecca J. Hester
Photo Stylists - Karen Hall and Cassie Newsome

PRINTED WITH SOYINK
Made in U.S.A.

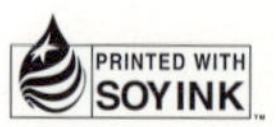

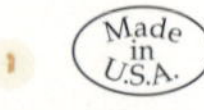